LANDMARKS IN MY COMMUNITY

THE AIRPORT

BY SADIE SILVA

Gareth Stevens PUBLISHING

Please visit our website, www.garethstevens.com. For a free color catalog of all our high-quality books, call toll free 1-800-542-2595 or fax 1-877-542-2596.

Library of Congress Cataloging-in-Publication Data
Names: Silva, Sadie, author.
Title: The airport / Sadie Silva.
Description: Buffalo, NY : Gareth Stevens, [2025] | Series: Landmarks in my community | Includes bibliographical references and index.
Identifiers: LCCN 2023034771 (print) | LCCN 2023034772 (ebook) | ISBN 9781538293072 (library binding) | ISBN 9781538293065 (paperback) | ISBN 9781538293089 (ebook)
Subjects: LCSH: Airports–Juvenile literature.
Classification: LCC TL725.15 .S55 2025 (print) | LCC TL725.15 (ebook) | DDC 387.7/36–dc23/eng/20230823
LC record available at https://lccn.loc.gov/2023034771
LC ebook record available at https://lccn.loc.gov/2023034772

Published in 2025 by
Gareth Stevens Publishing
2544 Clinton Street
Buffalo, NY 14224

Designer: Andrea Davison-Bartolotta
Editor: Caitie McAneney

Photo credits: Cover, p. 1 Lina Moiseienko/iStockphoto.com; series art (page numbers) art_of_sun/Shutterstock.com; series art (map background) Marian Salabai/Shutterstock.com; p. 5 muratart/Shutterstock.com; p. 7 Shine Nucha/Shutterstock.com; p. 9 Lukas Gojda/Shutterstock.com; p. 11 Andrew Angelov/Shutterstock.com; p. 13 Shine Nucha/Shutterstock.com; p. 15 Sailorr/Shutterstock.com; p. 17 PeopleImages.com - Yuri A/Shutterstock.com; p. 19 Gorodenkoff/Shutterstock.com; p. 21 William Perugini/Shutterstock.com.

Printed in the United States of America

CPSIA compliance information: Batch #CS25GS: For further information contact Gareth Stevens, New York, New York at 1-800-542-2595.

CONTENTS

Boldface words appear in the glossary.

Time for Takeoff!

Imagine a plane flying over you. It's taking people from one place to another. Some people fly on planes for work. Some people fly on planes for **vacation**. Either way, their **journey** begins at the airport!

What's an Airport?

Airports are important places in a community. They are the places where planes take off and land. Airplanes are kept and fixed there too. Some communities have big airports. Some communities have small airports. They help people **travel** near and far.

Let's Look at Airports

Many airports have buildings where people check in for their flight and get ready to board the plane. They also have runways. These are long stretches of flat ground. Airplanes take off from the runway.

RUNWAY

Visiting an Airport

You usually won't visit an airport unless you are traveling somewhere. You need a plane ticket. Some travelers go to big airports to travel out of the country. Some travelers go to small airports to travel within their country.

On the Job

Many people work in an airport. Some people work in **security**. Some people put bags onto the plane. Pilots fly the planes and go from airport to airport. Air traffic controllers direct the pilots. Flight attendants help people on the plane.

EXIT
FLIGHT ATTENDANT

What Happens There?

Once you get to an airport, you go to security. They check your bags and ticket. Then you go to a **terminal**. You wait for your plane and then board it. The plane **taxis** on the runway. Then it flies!

30

An Important Place

Not every community has an airport. Some people need to drive or take a bus to the nearest one. However, it is always an important part of a community. It **connects** people to other communities!

Airports allow people to live in one place but travel to another for work or visits. Without airports, people would have to stay in one place or drive very far. Also, airports **provide** jobs for people in the community.

AIR TRAFFIC CONTROLLERS

Your Community Airport

You can visit your community's airport to watch the planes take off, even if you can't go inside the terminal. Do you have an airport nearby? Is it big or small? Think about how the airport makes a difference in your community!

GLOSSARY

connect: To join together.

journey: A long trip from one place to another.

provide: To give.

security: A group whose main job is keeping a place safe.

taxi: To travel slowly on the ground before taking off or after landing.

terminal: A station for planes, trains, ships, or buses.

travel: To go from place to place.

vacation: A trip taken for fun and rest.

FOR MORE INFORMATION

BOOKS

Minden, Cecilia, and Mary Minden-Zins. *Pilots.* Parker, CO: Wonder Books, 2022.

Washburne, Sophie. *Great Airplane Designs.* New York, NY: Cavendish Square Publishing, 2023.

WEBSITES

Airplane
kids.britannica.com/kids/article/airplane/352719
Learn more about airplanes, including their history and use.

Airport Safety
www.funkidslive.com/learn/behind-scenes-airport/airport-safety/
Discover how one airport keeps their passengers safe while traveling.

Publisher's note to educators and parents: Our editors have carefully reviewed these websites to ensure that they are suitable for students. Many websites change frequently, however, and we cannot guarantee that a site's future contents will continue to meet our high standards of quality and educational value. Be advised that students should be closely supervised whenever they access the internet.

INDEX